WHAT I BELIEVE

A

WHAT I BELIEVE

by

R. LEONARD SMALL

THE SAINT ANDREW PRESS
EDINBURGH

© R. LEONARD SMALL 1970

First published in 1970
by The Saint Andrew Press
121 George Street, Edinburgh EH2 4YN
Reprinted April 1971

ISBN: 0 7152 0156 5

Printed by
William Blackwood & Sons Limited, Edinburgh

PREFACE

By the Rev. Dr. Ronald Falconer,
BBC Producer, " What I Believe ".

BBC-Scotland, so far as we know, is the only part of the world in which the religious television lecture flourishes—although the Australian Broadcasting Commission has relayed these Scottish lectures more than once with considerable accept-ance. " What ! " say the pundits. " A man talking religion in front of cameras ! Bad television and a shocking mis-use of the medium ! " The answer to that one is, " It depends upon the kind of man he is—and what he has to say ". He must be a person who can communicate at the deepest levels —but only a very few can do this with real impact.

A dozen years ago Dr. Hugh Douglas established the one-man television series with his helpful " Coping with Life " pastoral programmes. Professor William Barclay carried it on with his dynamic New Testament Lectures. During Lent 1970, Dr. Leonard Small gave the first series on Christian Belief, based on, equally, the Apostles' Creed and his own rich experience of the pastoral ministry. His " What I Believe " proved to be so popular that letters flowed in to us in the BBC and to Dr. Small himself. Viewers welcomed his positive instruction of the pattern of belief. Many said they were weary of being told what they could not, or should not believe. And they have a point. Our age questions every-thing—rightly !—but is so much better at pulling things down than building them up. By far the deepest reactions came from people writing out of agonizing personal situations of failure and tragedy. Dr. Small had to write literally hundreds of personal letters to such people, most of all on the two themes " The Forgiveness of Sins " and " The Life Everlasting "— the two themes, significantly enough, on which the Church preaches least nowadays.

As the reader will discover, " What I Believe " is positive Christian teaching coming straight out of the lives of ordinary men and women and supported by a first-class brain and the warmest of hearts. These talks were hammered out in the homes of anxiety and tragedy ; in hospital wards ; at business men's meetings and youth groups ; in the wide variety of situations of joy and sorrow in which Dr. Small has ministered to men and women " in sickness and in health ". I am delighted that the Saint Andrew Press is now making them available in this more permanent form.

CONTENTS

ACKNOWLEDGMENTS

The author and publisher acknowledge with appreciation permission to quote from the following copyright sources:

The extract from the poem " The Creation " is from *God's Trombones* by James Weldon Johnson. Copyright 1927 by The Viking Press, Inc., renewed 1955 by Grace Nail Johnson. Reprinted by permission of The Viking Press, Inc.

The lines by G. A. Studdert-Kennedy are from the poems " The Psychologist " and " Well? " from *The Unutterable Beauty*. Reprinted by permission of Hodder and Stoughton Ltd.

ABOUT GOD THE FATHER ALMIGHTY

These six addresses bear the general title, " What I believe ". They are in no sense theological lectures, indeed it might be better to call them " Talks " ; for they do not come out of the background and context of abstract study. They arise out of one man's personal experience of nearly forty years as pastor and preacher, mostly in large and very varied congregations, dealing with real people of all sorts, in every kind of situation of joy or sorrow or just sheer ordinariness. They are " aimed " . . . if I may use the phrase . . . not at the intellectuals who want to debate, dissect and perhaps discard as unworthy of thinking people the faith long accepted in this so-called Christian land, but rather at the bulk of our ordinary folk who are uncertain what they believe, are affected more than they realize by the winds of change, and who genuinely want to know if there is still a faith to which they can hold, that is valid and relevant in our exciting and bewildering world. In that context it was felt it might be helpful if one man would have the nerve just to say what he believes, and this is all I am setting out to do. Naturally this will involve saying why I believe, and keeping coming back to Christ in whom I believe, and who is the centre of everything.

These talks are placed in the setting of the great phrases of the Apostles' Creed. Although it bears this title, the Creed does not go back to the Apostles themselves, though in its essential statements it can be traced back to pretty near A.D. 100. It is a classic statement of the Christian Faith, which has been used for all these centuries, and also used very widely in the whole Church all round the world.

It therefore provides a helpful framework for any state-

B

ment of belief, saving me from just unloading my own pet ideas, reminding us all of what we cannot gloss over or leave out, and challenging us to ask what are the fundamentals of the faith still. I have repeated the Creed on an average twice a Sunday for the past thirteen years in my own church, and every phrase of it has been earthed in the real situations I have been sharing with my people in the preceding week. I have had to ask: " What does ' I believe in the Resurrection of the body and the Life Everlasting ' mean to that mother whose child was smashed by a speeding car, or that man, back in church after watching his wife die agonizingly from inoperable cancer ? " It is all as rooted in reality as that.

We begin with the first statement: " I believe in God, the Father Almighty, Maker of heaven and earth ". I believe that the most deeply true statement about the nature of the universe, and of the place in it of our little earth and this human life is contained in the first four words of the Bible, " In the beginning, God . . . "; the introduction to the famous verses read from the space-ship circling the moon on Christmas Eve, 1968. I find myself believing this more rather than less, as the horizons widen further and further and the mystery grows ever greater. I personally believe in a far greater God than I did forty years ago. Let me develop this.

A year ago I was interviewing, privately and individually the members of my class for First Communicants. One of them, a teacher, said that she found it difficult to accept what it says in the beginning of Genesis about God creating the world in six days. Taken completely by surprise I could only say that I saw the stories in question (for there are two not one) as stating in marvellous poetic language the truth that God created the heavens and the earth, that all things come from him, and that he has given man a special place and responsibility in his world. Given that basic assumption I welcome with gratitude and ever-increasing wonder all that any scientist can tell me about the nature and extent of the universe, and about our human life, for he keeps on showing me an infinitely greater God.

I have been lucky enough to travel a great deal ; twice to Australia, visiting Perth, Adelaide, Melbourne, Sydney and Brisbane ; once to New Zealand for six months in Dunedin. I have sailed right round the world, out by Suez, back by Panama, touching at Egypt, Aden, India and Ceylon. I have been as far East as Singapore, Malaysia and Hong Kong and looked over into Red China ; six times in the U.S.A. and to most of the European countries. The more I see of the world, the more I marvel at its sheer size, variety and complexity. Distance, even in terms of our tiny earth is something you can take in only when you have actually gone from here to there.

For example, here in Scotland, we can look at a map of Australia, on a scale small enough to get on to one page of an atlas. It looks like a large island, when in fact it is a continent. I had not realized this until I found it took me almost a day to fly from Sydney to Perth. The same point is made in the true story of the Edinburgh man who cabled his old friend in San Francisco: " Can you meet my son, arriving in New York airport Monday ? " and got back the realistic reply: " Meet him yourself. You're nearer ".

Sailing back from New Zealand over the Pacific I had ten days and then twelve out of sight of land, one moonlit night after another, the empty ocean all around, the glory of the starlit sky overhead. I thought of David crying, " When I consider thy heavens the work of thy fingers, the moon and the stars which thou hast ordained ; What is man ? " David saw only a mass of stars ; we can measure and count, and—most recent marvel—go and see. Going to the moon is a marvellous achievement of scientific skill, technological know-how and sheer courage ; but don't let us forget that in the total scheme of things it means no more than dropping in on your next-door neighbour. Distance to the stars is measured in light years, and light travels at a speed of 186,000 miles a second. That's pretty fast—tick—tick—we've been round the world seven times and are nearly halfway round our eighth orbit ! Think what that means when you add it up to a year of seconds.

As we sailed from south to north we exchanged the Southern Cross for the familiar Plough pointing to the Pole Star. Now the Pole Star, by whose light so many for so long have steered their way by land or sea or in the air, is so far away that the guiding light we bless tonight left there 466 years ago ! My imagination boggles, but it all fills me with wonder. If we ever really pictured God as a benevolent old gentleman perched on a woolly cloud, that won't do any longer.

The same process of expanding wonder goes on if we look in the opposite direction, into the microscopic world. Quite invisible to the naked eye, whole worlds of knowledge, understanding, power and potential are being opened up to the seeking mind by new instruments of research. Ever the wonder grows. There is an assumption, widely made, that as a result of all these new processes in both directions we shall quite soon know all there is to know about everything, and that God is therefore progressively unnecessary. Well, consider this : "We are confronted with many more mysteries of nature today than when the age of scientific enlightenment began. With every new answer unfolded, science has consistently discovered at least three new questions." Now who do you think said that ? Dr. Wernher Von Braun, director of NASA research and developer of the rockets that first put men on the moon.

Let me give you one further instance of my theme of expanding wonder ; this one in terms of time not space. Last year an American surgeon gave me a piece of fossilized coral. How old is it ? 350 million years—give or take a few thousand years either way. Now a Creator who can work out, evolve, produce something as beautiful as this on such a time scale is an infinitely greater God than one who waves a wand and, hey-presto, things happen like a conjuring trick.

Let us continue in our process of growing wonder. In all creation there is nothing half as wonderful as this human life of ours. In my present congregation in the last thirteen years I have baptized well over 700 babies so my total for the forty years must be well over the 1,000. I never take into my arms a normal healthy child, a tiny, helpless, vulnerable bundle of powers and possibilities, without marvelling afresh at this ever-recurring miracle, far more cleverly and intricately made than any space-ship, this sheer mystery of individuality and personality ; and the more the experts tell us of the way our life works the more I marvel. Here is something that cannot be contained within the categories of any psychological theory or explained away in terms of electrical impulses and nothing more. Yes—I still believe, I believe more than ever and with an increasing sense of awe and wonder and sheer joy, in God, the Father Almighty, Maker of heaven and earth.

The moment we say that, we are recognizing that this is basically God's world, not man's to do with as he likes. All sorts of problems are suddenly seen in a new and shocking light. A few years ago I married to a member of our choir a famous naturalist, Dr. Fraser Darling. Last year, in giving the Reith Lectures, he stressed the urgency and vast scale of the problems of pollution. We take the atmosphere which surrounds our earth and is our peculiar heritage and blessing, the clean air that is essential to health, and we pollute it with issues of our industry, the fumes of our ever-increasing traffic. We put insecticides on our crops, chemical weedkillers on our fields. The rain washes them down into the rivers, the fish become affected, and the ospreys who nest in their pine tree below the Cairngorms, fish-eaters as they are, lay eggs that are infertile. How widely we interfere with nature, upset its balance, and what price may we have to pay. From the oil slicks that can befoul our beaches to the old, scrapped cars that keep on piling up—what a mess we make of God's world !

Still more serious is our use, or rather abuse, of raw

materials and natural resources. If this is God's world, what
presumption it is for the wealthy, technologically-developed
nations of the world to squabble over, grab for and exploit
so selfishly the oil, the coal, the gas, the ore, the copper, the
nickel, the rubber and all the rest we pillage to maintain our
affluent society ! And, of course, if we dare to call the
Creator also Father, what about the glaring contrasts within
the human family of the haves and have-nots, the dreadful
shameful waste of food in a starving world, either at the
personal level of carelessness, or in pursuit of some economic
policy to keep up prices ? With all the potential that man's
skill has now unlocked there could well be enough for us all,
given the readiness to care enough.

At the same time, let us remember what an inspiration and
incentive this belief can be to those who share in any way in
God's creative purpose ; the dam-builders and engineers who
make the desert blossom as the rose ; the doctors and
research workers who fight disease, and make it possible for
more and more to live full and normal and happy lives. One
of the most exciting, imaginative and skilful pieces of creative
civil engineering of which I know is in the Snowy Mountains
scheme, south of Canberra in Australia. In creating an

artificial lake, seven times the volume of Sydney Harbour, a
tunnel had to be bored, fourteen miles long through solid
rock right under a mountain range. Most careful surveys
were done and checked ; a shaft 1,000 feet deep was driven
down through the heart of the mountain right over the line
and to the exact level of the projected tunnel, and boring
began four ways, in from either end and outward both ways
from the foot of the shaft. When they broke through and
checks were made for level and alignment, the error in the
fourteen miles was one quarter inch ! What a marvellous
universe we live in to be as calculable as that, and what
incredible skill to be entrusted to man ! What a satisfaction
to feel that what I do with my little life is in the line of God's
purpose, and that my little effort is part of his grand de-
sign ! Yes, and how tragic that so much of our modern living

denies utterly to so many this quality of rewarding purpose.

There is nowhere in the whole of life where we are so clearly privileged to share in the creative purpose of God as in the creation of a new life, starting a child on his strange, miraculous journey towards being a distinctive human being. We talk about sex as if it were a purely physical or biological function, or as if it were merely a means to a particular kind of enjoyment which can be indulged in quite selfishly and often with a total lack of responsibility. Christians are often concerned, and rightly, about the taking of life, as the question arises in relation to problems like war, or capital punishment, or euthanasia. Should we not be as much concerned, with all reverence, and responsibility, over the creation of life, and see in this setting questions so vexed as those of contraception and abortion ?

We call the Maker of heaven and earth " Father ". That is not to create God in our own image. It is to use the distinctive word Jesus used for God. Indeed he never used any other name but " Father ". Looking at the universe, the world, my own life in the terms of wonder I have outlined, I might well believe in an impersonal power, a Divine Idea, a sort of Computer Mind. That would be to leave God so remote as to be utterly out of range. If we are to grasp anything of the greatness and glory of God we must use the best pictures we can find, and this personal picture of Father best answers the demands of mind and heart. When I use it I am entering a relationship with this great God, linking my littleness to his power, wisdom and majesty. When a year ago I put one hand through the sleeve of an incubator and baptized a tiny premature twin, weighing just over one pound, it suddenly came to me that the power that holds the stars in their places was localized in that little specialized box, latching on to that tiny, fragile life. I was daring to do this unbelievable thing in the name of Jesus and because of him. For, as we shall be seeing in our second talk, God has done just that for all of us. He became localized in Jesus, and that is the biggest wonder of the lot.

Now we are going to sum up all our far-ranging thoughts in something very simple, almost naïvely so, the words in which the Negro poet, James Weldon Johnson, expresses what God did in the Creation.

And God stepped out on space,
And He looked around and said,
" I'm lonely—
I'll make me a world."

And God looked around
On all that He had made.
And God said, " I'm lonely still."

And the great God Almighty,
Who lit the sun and fixed it in the sky,
Who flung the stars to the most far corner of the night,
Who rounded the earth in the middle of His hand—
This Great God
Like a mammy bending over her baby,
Kneeled down in the dust
Toiling over a lump of clay
Till He shaped it in His own image ;
Then into it He blew the breath of life,
And man became a living soul.

2

ABOUT JESUS CHRIST

We started out in our first talk with God the Creator of the heavens and the earth, and we ended up by calling him "Father". Our thought soared way out into the unimaginable frontiers of the universe, and then came back to earth in the tiny box of an incubator. The Psalmist did the same long ago when he said: "He counts the number of the stars; he healeth the broken in heart" and we sing today:

> Centre and soul of every sphere,
> Yet to each loving heart how near !

Now how can we justify such a feat of mental gymnastics, how make sense of such a leap of faith ?

Paul put it best of all in a phrase that has a ring of trumpets about it: "God, who commanded the light to shine out of darkness, hath shined in our hearts, to give the light of the knowledge of the glory of God in the face of Jesus Christ." That glowing text makes me think of the basic principle of the camera—if you take a bright enough light and let it shine in through the lens on to a sensitized surface you will produce in the heart of the camera an image of the object on which the camera is focused, and this image can be faithfully reproduced. I believe that God, the great, mysterious God, whom no one has seen at any time, has given us in the face of Jesus Christ a true and living picture of himself as he really is. This is basic and central to all I believe. I start from this. I look outward from this and see at the heart of the universe not measureless might, nor unimaginable wisdom but love without limit. I look round on my world and view it with honest realism and unquenchable hope. I look in at my own life and I see it as it is, as it ought to be, and as it can yet become. So the first great phrase in the Creed marches me straight on, without a break, to what I believe about, and why I believe in, Jesus Christ: "Jesus Christ his only Son our Lord".

Notice at the outset how this familiar phrase sets a principle for all our thinking about Jesus Christ. We say in the same breath " his only Son " and " our Lord ". He belongs to God and to us. He belongs on God's side of things, and equally on ours. We must always hold these two aspects of him in focus, keep them in balance, or we go dangerously wrong. During World War II, I had often to do a Christmas Message in a crowded cinema, and it meant standing at the side of the stage in the shadows watching the screen, usually till the big picture finished. What a grotesque caricature I saw, looking from the side like that; the most glamorous actress was all elongated and out of shape. It didn't matter at which side I stood, the same thing happened. It was only those who sat out front, as near the centre as possible, who got a true and balanced picture. This is what we have to guard against, getting a one-sided picture of Jesus, going too far to one side or the other; if we do that, we always go dangerously wrong.

Begin with his name. He was called " Jesus " which was a quite normal Jewish name; it was the Greek equivalent of the Hebrew name Joshua; and they both meant " Deliverer " or, to use the New Testament word, " Saviour ". Now why should a deliverer or saviour be needed? Didn't our Negro poet picture God looking at each stage of his creation and saying " That's good " ? And did he not say it with the highest joy and satisfaction of the crown of his creation, man ? What had gone wrong with the world God made, and man to whom he had given dominion ? Something had got into the works. God had taken the appalling risk of making man not a puppet but a person entrusted with freewill, and everything had gone wrong. The story of the Fall is an imaginative attempt to explain the world as we know it to be, full of evil, sin, cruelty, injustice. It is a very penetrating study of the nature of sin, temptation and a sense of guilt. It had become painfully clear, as it is clearer than ever today,

that the world was not going to save itself, and God, because
he is love, could not stand apart, or write off the human
story as an experiment that failed. So he made plans for
"Expedition Rescue" (or, if you prefer religious language,
"Salvation"), slowly, patiently; much more slowly, patiently,
meticulously both in strategy and finest detail than all the
planning for D Day. Then, when the fulness of the time was
come, when everything was right—just as D Day depended
on the tide and the moon and the dropping of the wind—at
his selected bridgehead in Bethlehem of Judea, God launched
his invasion, so fantastically improbable as to be beyond
human invention. God came to save. But, again, there were
two sides to all this. The world could only be saved from
the inside, so God must be totally involved in our human
situation, really share our lot. If you see a non-swimmer
struggling in a flooded river you do not save him by standing
on the bank and shouting advice. You have to jump in and
risk being drowned yourself. In Jesus, fully human, sharing
our lot completely, I see God getting himself involved
totally in our situation, chewed into the machinery of
circumstance, crowded out into a stable because of a
Roman census at the beginning, hustled out of a crowded
city to public execution at the end, belonging among the
refugees, the displaced persons, the second-class citizens of
limited rights, the under-privileged. And this, let us never
forget, is all for real. This is no mere playing a part. H. G.
Wells used this awful description of Jesus: "He wears His
incarnation like a fancy dress". How wickedly untrue to
the real story. A business man may get fun out of dressing
up as a pirate for the office dance, cutlass and skull and
crossbones all complete, but he doesn't carry it through to
being hanged at the yardarm! Jesus is involved right to the
bitterest of bitter ends, no exemption, no merciful anaesthetic
at the last.

But the other extreme, getting too far out the other way is
just as bad, and in the climate of thought today is much more
tempting. The world can never be saved from the outside ;

but it is equally true that it will never be saved merely from the inside. All the new powers we possess, the fabulous know-how at our disposal, our undoubted cleverness, look more like destroying us than saving us. That is why we must still keep somehow the essential idea behind the old picture of being saved from above, from outside ourselves. This may sound terribly square, but I'm not helped by the picture of my own life and the world being saved, lifted into freedom and fulness, by some power discovered deep down inside myself, in God as the ground of my being, and working like a compressed air lift, as my car is lifted up for inspection. I still unrepentantly picture instead a man in a tiny rubber dinghy, lost for long enough as a tiny speck in a waste of tumbling waves. Now he's been spotted and the helicopter is hovering over him, but he is too chilled and weakened by long exposure to be able at all to fasten a safety harness round himself. A rescuer has to be lowered down beside him, fasten his limp body in the harness and clasp him as the winch up above takes the strain and they are hoisted together to safety. This is why it matters to me that this Jesus of Nazareth who lived only thirty-three years so long ago is also called " Christ ". That is the Greek translation of the Hebrew " Messiah " ; the one who was to come from God, the long-promised, long-awaited Deliverer. The hopes and fears of all the years were met in tiny Bethlehem that night so long ago, and keep on meeting there, for this, to me, is the story of God in action, doing something for us we could never do for ourselves, something that can never be undone, and will never need to be done again. God loved, God gave, God sent—all these are true, but I go beyond that.

The Queen usually sends to the General Assembly of the Church of Scotland her representative, the Lord High Commissioner. In 1969 she came herself. I believe that Jesus was not only God's special representative. In a very wonderful sense, in him God came himself. When anyone asks me to accept that Jesus was a very good man, even the finest man that ever lived, a religious genius, a masterly teacher,

the man for others who loved as no one else has ever loved—
that he was that and nothing more—I feel cheated and
deprived. That is to take from me the reality behind the
rescuer, the safety harness, the cable that will stand any
strain, the lifting winch, the presence and the power to save
that are God's alone.

All this is very sweeping and general, I very well know,
but it seems to be basic. It leads on naturally to the question
how we can picture the personality of Jesus belonging both
to God and man, sharing equally both natures. This is where
the phrase " was conceived by the Holy Ghost, born of the
Virgin Mary " comes in and must be faced. That there are
difficulties about the doctrine of the Virgin Birth cannot be
denied. More and more people seem prepared to discard it
as not belonging among the essentials of the faith. Professor
William Barclay discusses the problems very fully and fairly
in his book The Plain Man looks at the Apostles' Creed. He
points out the questions that arise regarding the direct refer-
ences in Matthew and Luke, the silence of the rest of the
New Testament, and the theological difficulties it raises.
While rightly leaving the question open for each individual
to decide, he himself rejects the idea, mainly on the grounds
that it leaves us with an incomplete incarnation, makes Jesus
essentially different from ourselves, and no longer our
example. For myself, I still accept it, because it seems to
express better than any alternative, certain fundamental ideas
in a great mystery.

Amid all the mystery I find myself searching for some
concept that will express the idea of two natures blended
into one personality, and I find it in the daily miracle of a
child, the belonger-to-both, the bridge between their separate
natures, with something of the heredity of each. I cling to
the belief that there was no time in the whole life of Jesus
when he was not revealing what God is like. That the
Creator of the ends of the earth should begin to reveal himself in the tiny invisible beginning of creation of a new life
at the moment of conception is humility greater even than

the birth in a stable. We call him God's *only* Son, and we are accepting that he stands in a quite unique relationship to God. He is one of us, bone of our bone, and flesh of our flesh, and yet he is different. To say that it is better to believe that the Spirit of God was uniquely operative at his birth in the normal way to Joseph and Mary—is this not suggesting a difference only in degree and not in kind? At Christmas we sing our hearts out in "O come all ye faithful" and we say of Jesus that he was "not made but begotten". What do we really mean? Some years ago I was visiting a young couple whose baby I had recently christened. They were perplexed by a Jehovah's Witness who insisted that Jesus was only the greatest of God's creatures, not in any sense his son. The young father was a joiner, and he had just made a beautiful tea-trolley, lovingly finished and polished. Pointing to it I said: "That is the creation of your hands, you made it. That baby in the cot is your only-begotten son. There is a difference." However we express it, don't let us lose the difference, the challenging sense of the uniqueness of Jesus Christ, about which we are getting so accommodating and apologetic.

All of this may seem very theoretical. To me it is crucially important what I can believe about this Jesus Christ. I say that as a minister. Suppose this Jesus is only a man like ourselves, a very good man, a man who had some brilliant ideas about God, the most totally loving man who ever lived —that and nothing more. Then what have I to say to a mother whose child has been killed in a road accident or has died of leukaemia, and who is wondering in her agony of mind and heart if there is a God at all, and if so what is he like? Is he callous, cruel, uncaring and unheeding, sitting up in heaven and letting things like that happen; or right in the centre of her agony, taking the hurt into his own heart? What have I to offer someone beaten by life into a sense of utter worthlessness? I cannot say that God in Christ is touching that life to uplift and transform it. How am I to help a man who has been unfaithful to his wife, imperilled the family he really loves, and who, although his wife has freely forgiven him cannot forgive himself? You see the enemies of Jesus objected to him saying to a crippled man " Your sins are forgiven " for only God could forgive sins. Were they not right, and how can the best of good men impart assurance of forgiveness?

For myself, just as a person, I only know that the God I see in Jesus Christ totally satisfies every demand of my mind and heart. If God is like that, then I can go on. I also know that this Jesus confronts and shames me as only God could do, and that he challenges and claims me as only God has any right to do. The very simplest form of creed of which there is the very earliest record in the story of the Church said merely this: " Jesus Christ is Lord ". This I totally accept. It stands at the heart of what I believe.

3

ABOUT JESUS CHRIST CRUCIFIED

I wonder if you happened to see, on film or television, or in actual reality, any of the samples of moon rock which the astronauts in Apollo 11 brought back with them. To me they seemed a very meagre result to be achieved at the cost of so much money, skill and effort, but the experts seemed to think they were worth it all. After all the various theories that had been propounded, they now know what the moon is really like, and they can draw their own wider conclusions.

In this third talk, we are setting out to explore a whole world of mystery, where the minds of men have been searching for 2,000 years, and they still have not found the final answer to the questions that arise. Look at the ground we have to cover : " Suffered under Pontius Pilate, was crucified, dead and buried ; he descended into hell ; the third day he rose again from the dead ; he ascended into heaven and sitteth on the right hand of God, the Father Almighty ; from thence he shall come to judge the quick and the dead ". How can we hope to do any more than pick up a few handfuls from the surface of all this, and trust that they will prove to be what we can grasp, both true and typical of a reality that baffles all our wisdom and eludes our understanding ?

We begin then with " Suffered under Pontius Pilate ". Strange that nothing else is said of the whole earthly life of Jesus, lasting thirty-three years, than just this. It seems as if the early Church in which the Creed took shape felt that what mattered most to record was that Jesus suffered. The word " suffered " is itself significant. The Latin of it means literally " to get underneath in order to carry a load ", " to bear up from below ". The Basic English of it is " to undergo ". In my boyhood I knew a man, a sturdy Borderer, endowed with broad shoulders and unusually long arms. He was a joiner and builder, and one day he came upon two

of his men working on a building site. They were having a
great job with an awkward boulder. They would lever away
with their crowbars, and always at the last moment it would
slip back into its hole. My friend pushed them aside and
climbed down into the hole. Straddling the boulder he
worked his long arms little by little beneath it, always lifting
a little till his fingers interlocked underneath. Then he
straightened his shoulders and gradually drew it up on to his
knees, pivoted on his heels and with a final heave tipped it
safely out of the way. Trying to disguise his satisfaction at
this feat of strength, he dusted his hands and clothes and
remarked, almost casually, " I dinna ken what all the fuss
was aboot ! " Perhaps the framers of the Creed were sum-
ming up the entire process of the Incarnation when they
said " Suffered ", for was not Christ's whole life an ever-
increasing getting down below all our human burdens, that
he might take them upon himself ?

" Under Pontius Pilate " reminds me . . . and I need to be
reminded, more than ever . . . that what I believe is grounded
in history. There is a lot of loose talk about the Gospel
accounts of the life of Jesus as if they belonged obviously in
the realm of myth, legend and fairy-tale. But they are not
so written. They are dated, and located, both geographically
and historically, and tied to the names of real persons, such
as Herod or Pilate. I like this solid feel of history. It
steadies me when someone suggests that my belief in Christ
is on the level of a growing child going on believing in Santa
Claus and that I am only kidding myself on. No, I am
dealing with what purport to be historical facts, and the
specific singling out of Pilate recalls me to a sense of the
nature of my responsibility now I have got this far in setting
down what I believe. Why is Pilate singled out like this
when it was Judas that betrayed, the chief priests that plotted
and forced the issue, the crowd who howled for Barabbas ?
Pilate thought Jesus was innocent and repeatedly said so, but
it was he who condemned him at last, for no one else could
do so.

C

Pilate's bewildered question echoes down the corridors of time: "What shall I do with Jesus?" He gave his own wrong answer and he is stuck with the blame so long as the Creed is said. He reminds me, and you and all of us that, now we have got this length, what matters is not what we think about but what we do with this Jesus.

The record moves on, as inexorably as the procession to Calvary itself: "Was crucified, dead and buried". The crucifixion of Jesus Christ must surely be the most widely known public execution in all history. To all of the world's 700 million Roman Catholics the crucifix, large or small, is a central object of devotion, and to all the rest of us, whatever our difference in doctrine, the Cross is a focal point of our faith. Beneath the Cross of Jesus we all must take our stand if we start thinking about him at all. What are we to see there? Around this scene the artists, the sculptors, the music-makers, have gathered the instruments of their skill. On this they have lavished—sometimes for rich reward, often as the outpouring of their own devotion—their art, often amounting to genius. Sometimes the grimness has been emphasised, the lacerated wounds, the thorn-torn brow, the pierced side, and we have built up a kind of immunity against it. Sometimes the reality has been obscured by the decoration of devotion. Let us try to come at it afresh, as far as we can.

Why was Jesus crucified? Why did he die, and die like that? We have once again to hold two thoughts in balance. He died because his enemies hated and feared him, the religious, political, commercial and military leaders wanted rid of him. But he died also because he chose to do so. In his own words: "No man taketh my life from me, but I lay it down of myself". He died a victim of human cruelty; hatred, falsehood, blind prejudice set a trap for him, and Judas sprung the trap; but the victim had walked into it with his eyes open. Even when he is caught, his hands tied, even nailed to the Cross, one is left with the strange impression that the victim is victor; it is he who is judging Herod,

Caiaphas, Pilate and the rest, not they him. What we are seeing is a show-down, a trial of strength between the power of sin and evil with all the worst that they can do, and the strange power of love that goes on loving to the end.

Keep on watching and it becomes clear that he is not dying for his own sins, for anything he has done. The charges against him are trumped up, and the Jewish trial is a tissue of illegalities. Pilate, an experienced and competent judge of true and false, repeatedly declared him innocent ; the dying thief bore his own witness, " This man hath done nothing amiss ". He is dying like that for the sins of others, at least " for " in the sense of " because of ". But now we are being led down deeper. When we were children most of us sang, in the words of Mrs. Alexander's famous hymn:

> We may not know, we cannot tell,
> What pains he had to bear ,
> But we believe it was for us
> He hung and suffered there.

But if we think about it we can understand a little of what it meant to him.

First there was the pain of anticipation ; Jesus clearly foretold his death and the manner of it. Remember he had seen men crucified, and knew exactly what it meant. If you have ever waited for an operation so critical that it was clearly a matter of life and death, and either way a horrible experience, you know something of the agony of anticipation. Or to be even more realistic, recent discussion on capital punishment has set before us the feelings of a man awaiting execution ; from the moment Jesus set his face like a flint to go to Jerusalem he was in the condemned cell and knew it. Think of the build up of Holy Week, the mental and spiritual agony, the sheer physical horror of the scourging, the crucifixion itself, not just the initial shock of the nails driven through flesh and nerves, but the lingering agony that followed. Sum it all up in that cry of dereliction, cut off even from God. Are we beginning to know a tiny fraction

of the pains he had to bear, and coming nearer to the heart
of the mystery ? Yet none of this is merely being inflicted on
him. He is taking it into his own heart; the lies and the
hatred of the leaders of religion, the pathetic vacillation of
Pilate, the brutal buffoonery of the soldiers, their callous
execution of a familiar duty. He is taking it all into his own
heart, thinking not of what they are doing to him, but what
they are doing to themselves. That is why he prays,
" Father, forgive them for they know not what they do ".

Does the phrase " dying for the sins of others " begin to
take on a new shade of meaning ? The strange fact about
the Cross is that it produces a feeling of involvement as does
no other story of a sacrificial death, however noble or tragic.
Merely reading the story, hearing it sung to the music of
Bach, seeing it magnificently portrayed on the stage at
Oberammergau, one ceases to be a spectator and is drawn in.
The haunting question: " Were you there when they crucified
my Lord ? " has only one possible answer. Men have tried
very hard to put into theological theories what happened at
the Cross ; they have used the language of the market and
hinted at a bargain between Jesus and God, so that the wrath
of God was bought off, or they have changed to the law-
courts and suggested the Judge paying the penalty he himself
has imposed, but these are only broken fragments of the
mystery.

For myself, there are three realities that stand out. At the
Cross as nowhere else I see what sin can do, not the sin of
rare monsters of iniquity, but just sins like mine ; my pride
and jealousy, my fears and prejudices, the untruths that are
part of me. I see them raised to the nth power. I see what
they can do to God. At long last I am shocked into hating
them and wanting to be free. I see in Jesus dying there the
length to which God is prepared to go to set me free, and I
bow before the irresistible compulsion of love that never
gives up, never gives in, keeps on loving to the last. In the
whole story of all Jesus suffered I see there is no experience
of trial or testing, of torture and agony to body, mind or

spirit I shall ever be called to undergo, where the love of
God will not be there before and about me. " He leads us
through no darker rooms than he has gone before." I move
on with wonder and gratitude to that last cry out of total
darkness: " My God, why ? " because so often I have to
listen to people uttering that cry, and share it with them. I
know that even when I see nothing but darkness, the love of
God is still there. Amid all the maze of theological specu-
lation, of these things I am sure.

We have spent a lot of time here, because it is literally
crucial. Now we move on, still in the same direction. " Dead
and buried " . . . you would almost think that phrase was put
in, as it may well have been, to refute one of the many
attempts to " explain away " the awkward fact of the Resurrection, namely the suggestion that Jesus was not really dead,
but had only swooned, and in the cold of the grave recovered
and somehow made his way out and returned to the disciples.
This theory really makes no sort of sense, and is untrue to
the records which make it quite plain that he conveyed to
the disciples the impression that he had not merely survived
death but had conquered it. Put together the whole phrase
" was crucified, dead and buried " and these words sound
'like nails driven home in a coffin lid," making it quite clear
that Jesus was really and truly dead. They also round off
the whole movement and process of the Incarnation, for they
assure us that Jesus truly shared our human lot, right to the
bitter end. He faced up to our every enemy, including
the last enemy, death. Some of us are more fortunate than
others ; we do not need so badly his help, because we do
not undergo all the experiences he went through for our
sakes. But it is interesting that there is just one fact of
which at this moment every one of us can be completely and
absolutely sure, and that is that we shall all one day die.
This phrase assures me that Jesus has gone through that
darkest of all dark rooms.

I sometimes find it helpful to draw the pattern of the story
of Jesus' life in terms of a graph, and it works out as a down-

ward curve. Begin, if you like, with " He came down to earth from heaven " or " Who, being very and eternal God, came down from heaven in perfect love and became man ". The beginning of the life itself was a coming down, being born below the human level among the animals. His whole life was a steady coming down to our level, however mean, lowly and ordinary. At his baptism he went down into the water bowing down to take on himself the biggest burden of all, our human sin. He went on going down lower and lower, even unto death and the grave. Could he go even lower still ? This is where I set the strange, perplexing idea apparently contained in the phrase " He descended into hell ". We *must* understand that " hell " in this phrase does not mean what we normally accept it to mean, a place of fire and everlasting torment and punishment.

The Jews believed that at death the souls of men went into a strange kind of in-between state, which was not utter extinction on the one hand, nor was it fully living on the other. It was situated " under the earth " and was variously known as " The place of dead ", " Hades " or " Hell ". In this strange shadowy world were held the dead of all generations. That is the setting of this part of the Creed as it originated, and of course it makes no sort of sense in terms of our modern understanding of the world and of life. But may not this old idea still be saying something important, even to us ?

If I am in a car crash and lie in hospital in a coma, in a condition described as " deeply unconscious " I may recover, and return, if I am very fortunate, to normal life. I have no recollection of that period . . . where have " I " been ? In the expanding realm of organ transplant it is more than ever important to determine the point of death. This is done no longer in terms of the heartbeat stopping—that can be artificially re-started ; what is decisive is the response of the brain to electrical stimuli. When that stops I am dead ; where do " I " go ?

No one can tell me, but this old phrase assures me that

into whatever dark experience I may ever have to go, I will always meet the love of God in Christ coming up from lower down still. There is another shade of meaning here to which I find it worthwhile to cling. In one of the Epistles of Peter there is a strange text, trying to explain where Jesus went, and what he was doing between the moment of his death on the Cross and the glory of Easter morning. It says: "He went and preached to the spirits in prison". In other words he carried out a special mission to all the generations who had lived and died too soon, and had never had a chance to hear his gospel of the love of God. In a world where we are rightly sensitive about discrimination of any sort isn't this a real issue? If we believe that the response a man makes to the offer and challenge of God in Jesus Christ is truly a matter of life and death, and makes an eternal difference, is not this unfair to those who never had the chance, and here and now never get it? Fanciful, you say? Maybe, I only know I welcome any hint that the love of God is big enough and wise enough not to leave anyone out.

Now, suddenly, dramatically, the curve of our graph turns and sweeps steeply and gloriously upwards, with the story of the Resurrection and all that followed. Here, once again, we enter a realm of current controversy, of divided opinion, even, almost, of new heresy hunts. Into none of those do I propose to enter, but I shall be content to state positively my own position. There are problems which arise regarding the variations in the records of the appearances of the risen Christ. Some say in Jersusalem, some in Galilee. There is a question mark about the evidence of the empty tomb, which is not mentioned at all by Paul in the earliest list of appearances in I Corinthians, 15, nor in Mark, the earliest of the Gospels. What is not in question is that the Gospels and the book of Acts convey the impression of an incredible transformation in the disciples. Something happened between the Friday night and the evening of Easter Sunday to change them from a terrified group of deserters, leaderless, starting at every sound, to men of such courage, determination and unquenchable faith that they withstood everything the Jewish leaders could do to silence them. On the Friday night they were shocked into helplessness by the death of Jesus ; Peter, who might have rallied them, was off somewhere in the bottomless abyss of his shame.

Something happened in what has been called " thirty-six hours that changed the world ". For within days these same disciples were out in the streets of Jerusalem, with Caiaphas and Annas and all the rest still in power, declaring that Jesus had arisen from the dead, and getting people to believe them. No one has ever yet explained away this change, quite out of character, and for me it is basic. From it much follows. The New Testament itself is witness to the Resurrection: the joy and triumph of the Resurrection ring through it from first to last ; it thrills and vibrates with the presence and power of the living Christ. If Christ had died and stayed dead the story of this brief and tragic life would never have been written and I doubt if we would ever even have heard his name. The Church is witness to the Resurrection, for it was founded in its tiny, unlikely beginnings on belief in the risen Christ, and withstood persecution in the early days in the power of that belief. It has gone on growing and spreading in spite of cruel pressure from without and debilitating corruption from within. If Christ is not risen then Christianity is the biggest confidence trick in all history. K. S. Latourette, near the beginning of his monumental *History of Christianity,* says of this Jesus, " That life is the most influential ever lived on this planet and its effect continues to mount ". Quite a lot to be founded on a lie. Experience witnesses to the Resurrection. In forty years I have seen hundreds of people, of all sorts, face life with a radiance of joy, a tireless compassion for others and an unconquerable courage and faith which I can only explain by saying that Christ is alive for them, in them and through them. My own personal experience bears the same witness, for things have happened to me of such a nature that they left me with no option but to say: " Christ was there ". Not to believe this would be to me like looking in the mirror and not seeing my own face.

" The third day he rose again from the dead ; he ascended into heaven and sitteth on the right hand of God the Father Almighty ". Look how the graph keeps climbing and soaring till we are back where we began, with God the Father Almighty. But what can we make of all this in the space age, when "ascending" doesn't get you to heaven, and we just can't picture God any more sitting up there ? Well, before we write all this off let's stop to ask what these old pictures could be saying. The Ascension and exaltation, what are they but the vindication of Jesus and all he claimed to be and to do ? They are God's splendid "Yes" to all that Jesus stood for, lived for, died for. This that we see in Jesus is true and real. This is set at the heart of all things. Here is the fundamental reality of all existence. Here is the answer, with God's seal of genuineness on it, to the question raised at Calvary: " What kind of world are we living in anyway ? Do hatred, cruelty, falsehood, always win in the end ? " The last word is with love as we see it in Jesus.

Two minor by-products, fringe benefits, must be mentioned here. The Ascension in the New Testament marks the end of an era. After it there are no more appearances. He is not localized any more except wherever he is loved, needed, served. So I myself have prayed and spoken to him 35,000 feet up in an aircraft, and 300 feet down in a submarine ; and one of the most joyful and realistic Easter Services I have ever taken was on a liner between Sydney and Auckland, far far from Jerusalem, yet not from him. The sitting on the right hand could be our guarantee that our human lot will never be far from God's heart. God will never forget, so long as " he pleads our cause at God's right hand ".

Finally, what of the doctrine of the Second Coming ? To some Christians this is totally central ; to some it is on the circumference of their faith. What it stands for positively is that history is going somewhere. It is not just a vicious spiral. The end of all things will not be some holocaust in which all life is consumed, or a dead universe from which life has faded. It will be the final triumph of Christ. What is of immediate moment is that Christ keeps on coming to us as he said he would, and he must always come in judgment. Yet, remembering all that this talk has told us of the nature, the sharing, the caring of his love, who on the Cross prayed "Father, forgive them" I would still dare to say, in the very last words of the New Testament: "Even so . . . come, Lord Jesus".

4

ABOUT THE HOLY GHOST

We began our study of what we believe with God the Father
Almighty, Maker of heaven and earth. We followed the
story of what God did in Jesus as the Creed sweeps us on
from stage to stage, picturing the whole incredible process in
terms of our graph of the downward and upward curve. We
left it at the point of the vindication and triumph of Jesus,
as the story of the Ascension and exaltation seek to express
this essential climax to the whole drama of man's salvation.
Perhaps the point where we left off can best be marked by
the famous scene from John Masefield's play where the wife
of Pilate is asking the centurion in charge of the crucifixion
if he thinks Jesus is really dead. When he replies firmly:
" No, lady, I don't ", she goes on, quite naturally, to ask:
" Then where is he ? " He gives the challenging reply: " Let
loose in the world, lady, where neither Roman nor Jew can
stop his truth." It is from that splendid conviction to which
all I have said irresistibly leads me, that we start again on
the next stage. What happened afterwards ? For we realize
that the end is not yet in sight.

It is at this point, that, one might almost say, a third main
character appears on the scene in this drama. We have met
with God the Father, and Jesus Christ his only Son our
Lord ; in the next act a most prominent part is played by
the person who is introduced to us by the phrase in the
Creed: " I believe in the Holy Ghost ". We shall come back
to the question of how these three are related to each other.
At the outset we have to clear the ground. In my own
church we follow the common practice of having the younger
children in church only for the first part of the morning service, and they go out to Sunday School during the children's
hymn. At a recent Family Service, one small boy happened
to be in church for the first time through the entire service.
When we repeated the Creed and came to this phrase, he

nudged his father, in great excitement, as if something really interesting were at last happening in church and asked, " Daddy, is it a _real_ ghost ? " It is time we got rid of all the wrong associations of this title " Ghost ", which no longer means what it did when the Creed was first fashioned in English, and began afresh with the word " Spirit ", wiping the slate clean, as it were, and getting back to the great fundamental idea which confronts us here.

The word " spirit " occurs in the very first verses of the Bible, where it states that: " The earth was without form and void . . . and the spirit of God moved upon the face of the waters ". This is the beginning of life, movement, creation ; and the agent of God's activity is the Spirit. The Hebrew word is _ruah_ and it has two shades of meaning, both of them significant and suggestive. First, it can mean " the wind " and this is a helpful picture. You are sitting by the seashore on a day of flat calm, not a breath (significant expression!) is stirring. Or you are picnicking by the loch-side and the water is like glass, reflecting in a perfect mirror the sweep of the hillside, the trees, the whitewashed cottage, the black and white cattle, all upside down. Then, almost imperceptibly, the calm surface becomes ruffled, the clear image is blurred, and it grows colder. The wind has sprung up ; you cannot see it, but you can observe its effects. The cornfield moving and rippling like a golden sea, the tall pine trees pushed over as by an unseen hand . . . they offer the same image of an invisible power, perceptibly at work, and with this we can begin to understand the idea of the Spirit of God at work in the world in terms of activity and movement.

The other idea—that of " breath "—is not essentially different. The link can be simply made. If you are in a desperate hurry to drink up a cup of tea that is too hot, you can cool it down by the elementary if vulgar process of blowing on it. The effect you produce in your teacup is an exact miniature of the Spirit of God moving on the face of the waters. Then we move on to a new shade of idea. When

Genesis comes to the description of the creation of man, we
read: "God formed man of the dust of the ground, and
breathed into his nostrils the breath of life; and man became a living soul". Here then, we have the idea of the
Spirit of God breathing into human beings something of his
own life, or on occasion giving to them an extra quality of
living. "On occasion" is a relevant phrase, for in the Old
Testament generally the Spirit of God comes to special
people to endow them for a specific task, to enable a prophet
to speak fearlessly in God's name, or even, surprisingly, to
make possible Samson's superhuman feats of strength.
Always whichever picture we use, the Spirit is the unseen
agent of God's activity.

So we come to the New Testament, where the word for
"spirit" is the Greek word *pneuma* and it has precisely the
same two shades of meaning: "the wind" and "breath".
This is easy to recognize. If you ride a bicycle, you run on
tyres into which wind or air has been blown, or if you drive
a car, you would be wise to check the pressure of air in your
tyres, because both sorts are *pneumatic*. If you contract a
certain infection of your lungs, your breathing apparatus, you
probably have *pneumonia*. Here, then, we have these two
reasonably clear and simple pictures contained in the very
word for the Spirit.

When we look through the Gospels we see the Old Testament idea continued. The Spirit is the agent (and I use the
personal, human word "agent" rather than the impersonal,
almost mechanical word "instrument", advisedly) of God's
activity. The Spirit is uniquely, creatively active in the
conception of Jesus. The Spirit descends upon him at his
baptism. The Spirit drives him out into the wilderness to
be tempted. Once again we see the established principle of
the Spirit being given to special people for particular purposes, as, for example, when old Simeon came "by the
Spirit" to the Temple just at the right time to see his hopes
and dreams realized in the child Jesus.

Let us note, in passing, before we move on from the

Gospels, the phrase that is used to describe Jesus at the moment of his dying: " He gave up the ghost " ; " He yielded up the ghost ". Most interesting is the description given by Luke, alone: " Jesus said, ' Father, into thy hands I commend my spirit ' ; and having said thus, he gave up the ghost ". The noun translated " spirit " is our word *pneuma*, and the root of the verb " gave up the ghost " is also *pneuma* and means literally: " He breathed out his last breath ". So we can see the close connection between " ghost " or " spirit " and breath and life itself. Let's carry that forward with us as we think our way through to the beginning of Acts.

The story of the earthly life of Jesus is complete. He has lived among men for thirty-three years. He has died on the Cross, revealing the love of God as an inescapable reality and focusing it as a redeeming power on the lives of men. He has convinced his own that he has conquered death and is alive for evermore. Now the appearances have ended, he has gone away from them, but they are joyful rather than sad, for they know he has only gone, as Dr. Maltby has so finely said, " out of the here into the everywhere, away from some men's sight that He might come home to all men's hearts." So these men are not sad, for they know that, as he promised, they are not left like orphans. But they seem to be marking time, doing nothing, waiting for something to happen. They are waiting, according to instructions, for the next great creative act of God.

I find myself picturing a great modern factory, with its sophisticated machinery set up in all the different departments, and the skilled operators standing by each with his or her own expertise, but doing nothing yet, for the opening ceremony is about to be performed, and they are waiting perhaps, for some royal personage to throw the main switch. Once that is done the whole place begins to hum with planned and orderly activity.

That's how I tend to picture, in modern terms, the event we call Pentecost or Whit Sunday. Notice the details of the familiar description. "They were all with one accord in one place, and suddenly there came a sound from heaven as of a rushing mighty wind" . . . there's your Spirit of God moving on the face of the waters once again, creative activity . . . but look how the amount, the strength of the wind is stressed. No gentle zephyr this, no puff ruffling the surface for a moment and then dying away: no, indeed, it filled all the house where they were sitting. The picture is of enough and more than enough.

Then "there appeared unto them cloven tongues like as of fire, and it sat upon each of them"—fire, symbol of cleansing and inspiration. The very intriguing phrase "sat upon each of them" really means that the fire was distributed around—almost like dealing out a hand of fire—so that each got his own little tongue of flame. "And they were all filled with the Holy Spirit", as if each had breathed deeply into his own life this mighty wind, this new clear, pure revivifying air. The result was amazing. In terms of the famous advertisement they were "Plus an extra something the others hadn't got."

They and those who came after them found an extra on the physical level. Paul is the classic case of this. The story of this man, who was subject to recurring bouts of prostrating illness, travelled great distances, mostly on foot and in trying conditions, and endured stoning, flogging, shipwreck and frequent attempts on his life, must be just about an all-time record for sheer physical endurance. And he did it in the power of the Spirit.

They found an extra on the mental level. In the Gospels the disciples give the impression of being pretty dull-witted—slow in the uptak' to use a Scots phrase—certainly not particularly bright. Now they were quite different. Peter the fisherman who appeared to have a natural gift for handling any situation in a blundering way, and for saying the wrong thing, became a wise and astute leader.

He and the others found an extra on the level of the will. The Jewish authorities had to sit up and take notice when they came up against the boldness of Peter and John ; the same Peter who denied his Master at a servant lassie's casual remark !

They found an extra on the spiritual level. They were infinitely surer of God, trusting in his power, accepting his guidance, gloriously certain of his presence with them in the person of their risen Lord. They went out in the power of the Spirit to " out-think, out-live and out-die " the pagan world as Dr. T. R. Glover has said.

The new element in the situation, which becomes ever clearer as the Church begins to grow and spread, is that the Spirit, previously imparted only to special people for particular purposes, becomes the normal endowment of every Christian, as extra equipment for the tasks of ordinary living. This is where we come in, but before we look at the implications for ourselves of all this in the modern world, let us note two very important considerations that arise out of the New Testament idea of the Holy Spirit.

As we follow the unfolding story of the growth of the Church in the book of Acts it is abundantly clear that the Holy Spirit is regarded as not only personal but *a person*. The Spirit holds the centre of the stage, Director of Operations, almost Commander-in-Chief. This is most important for our thinking ; we must never fall into the error of picturing the Holy Spirit as a kind of diffused gas, or even some-*thing* laid on like the oxygen supply in a jet aircraft flying at 35,000 feet. The Holy Spirit is never " it ". The Holy Spirit is always " He ".

And that brings us inevitably bang up against what is for most of us the very difficult doctrine of the Trinity ; difficult, however often we may listen uncritically to the Benediction: " The grace of the Lord Jesus Christ, the love of God and the fellowship of the Holy Spirit be with you all ". It is most important to remember that this doctrine was not " cooked up " by some theologians to perplex us ordinary believers. This is no product of any ivory tower, but an attempt to interpret and systematize the experience of the

Church, what the ordinary believer sees happening in his own Christian life.

Most of the early Christians were Jews. They had grown up with the idea of the one God, Creator of heaven and earth, Lord of history, the Father Almighty, infinitely great, unsearchable in wisdom, outside their lives yet touching them in his providence and grace. The first disciples came to know God in a new and wonderful way as he came to them in Jesus, walking the roads with them, breaking bread, both common and sacramental, with them, becoming to them both Friend and Saviour. This relationship was not broken by his death but only entered on a new and wonderful stage, at which they were joined by all who came to accept him as Saviour and serve him as Lord. In addition they came, all of them alike, to find God at work in and through their lives by his indwelling Spirit. The idea of one God, Father, Son and Holy Spirit, one Person known in three different ways, made sense of their experience as it does of ours. We, too, know and experience God in these three ways, and this idea, for me, makes sense.

When I wrestle with the difficulty of worshipping three different Persons in some curious way rolled into one, I am helped by using the human parallel of one person known by different people in different aspects of his personality. Take, for example, some up-and-coming surgeon, operating excitingly in one of the developing fields of surgery, such as that of kidney transplants. His patients know him as the expert who can give the final verdict in what is a life-and-death situation. They see him as the kindly man who seems to understand and can therefore allay their fears; who explains to them what he must do and why he must do it; who by his manner and caring instils in them confidence and faith. He sees them before the operation. He takes their lives in his hands. He watches over them as they go through the slow process of adjustment and rehabilitation, and they are for ever grateful. When he goes home in the evening he may gladly relax, get down on the floor with his young sons

D

with their electric train set, link up carriages and trucks instead of arteries and muscle. These boys see him differently from the patients, but he is still the same man. Now let us imagine that, tired and over-strained, he takes a long week-end off, going with a friend from student days to a little fishing hotel at the back of beyond. We can imagine them sometimes catching fish, sometimes just fishing, sitting together in the evening, sometimes talking shop, sometimes yarning of this or that mutual interest. That old friend sees our surgeon differently again from his patients and his sons, but he is still the same person.

I don't know if this helps; if it does we have to go one stage further. With human personality there may be contrasting aspects of character, not quite " pavement saint, fireside devil " but you know what I mean. Hitler, with all his hideous public policies, was said to be a most gracious host to people he liked in his home at Berchtesgaden ! With God the Father, the Son, and the Holy Spirit all is in character. Between the grace of the Lord Jesus Christ, the love of God and the free, life-giving fellowship of the Holy Spirit, the common denominator, the prevailing trait of character, is love; love which in its length and breadth and depth and height we can never begin to understand.

What, then, does the Holy Spirit mean in our experience in this totally different world ? Can we find this extra that the Spirit is supposed to give, as we have said, to any Christian ? Let's begin with two very simple, down-to-earth examples.

Have you ever had the kind of experience you can only describe by saying: " Something said to me, ' Go and do so-and-so ' ? " This has happened to me dozens of times. I have been going about my ordinary business as a minister when something said to me: " Go and visit Mrs. X." As far as I knew Mrs. X didn't particularly need me, and what I was on my way to do was much more important, but the inner voice was so insistent I just had to turn and go. In every case without exception I was welcomed somewhat thus by each Mrs. X: " Thank God you've come. I need your help very badly, and I was praying you would come." One minister friend of mine had this experience, and resisted the inner voice most strenuously because his Mrs. X was a particularly difficult old lady. He finally gave in, went to her bungalow, could not get an answer, and broke in to find her lying in a gas-filled room, having turned on the gas to make a cup of tea and failed to light it. I believe the " something that said " was the Holy Spirit, directing a responsive human being to do something God wanted.

My other example is of the common experience of being upheld in some situation of strain and stress or sorrow and tragedy. Again and again people have said to me out of the agonizing heart of such a situation : " If you had told me I could endure what I have in fact gone through, I wouldn't have believed it. I can only say I have been brought through it. I have been given the strength just as and when I needed it." That, quite unquestionably, is the comfort of the Holy Spirit. Here is more than common human fortitude. This is that quite wonderful extra.

This raises another question ; that of being " tuned-in " to the Spirit. During World War II British agents parachuted into enemy-occupied territory, and usually joined forces with the underground movement. They used their transmitting radio sets to make contact with base in Britain to report enemy troop movements, to order and arrange supply drops and the like. This was done by broadcasting on a particular frequency at a pre-arranged time, which might vary according to plan to avoid risk of detection, and the assumption was that someone would be listening. How tragic if an agent took his life in his hands to send out a crucial message and got no response! I believe that the Holy Spirit is continually at work in our lives ; that

> Every virtue we possess
> And every victory won
> And every thought of holiness
> Are his alone.

But we need to be tuned in.

It's in that setting that I want to make a plea for the widening of the scope of our application and acceptance of the operation of the Holy Spirit. We accept that some whole-time dedicated Christian will be inspired, a minister now and then will preach an inspired sermon, a medical missionary will carry on crucial work even if desperately short-handed. When Handel wrote the entire score of the " Hallelujah Chorus " in the intensive effort of one day, and said he saw the heavens opened and God on the great white throne, this we accept as inspiration. Why stop there ? The Commonwealth Games in Edinburgh this summer make me think back to the Paris Olympics over forty years ago, when an Edinburgh student, Eric Liddell, was chosen to run in the 100 metres but withdrew because he refused to run in the heats on a Sunday. He switched to the 400 metres, somehow scraped through to the final and won the Gold Medal. Some of the very pressmen who had slanged him for his narrow-minded religious scruples said that he ran " like a man inspired " and asked how he managed it. He opened his hand and showed a sweaty screw of paper he had been clutching all through the race and said, " Somebody thrust that into my hand just before the start." On it was written a text: " Him that honoureth me I will honour ". Why can't we be more daring and imaginative in the scope we allow to the Holy Spirit if we really believe that God is concerned with the whole of life and not just the religious bits of it ?

I welcome most gladly a recent development in medical practice which helps me wonderfully to understand what we have been thinking about in this entire talk. When someone is pulled from the sea or lake or river apparently drowned you don't use the old laborious Schaefer method of artificial respiration. You lay the patient down in the proper position with the head held back and the nostrils covered. You put your lips to his lips. You breathe your breath of life into his lungs and go on breathing in and out until, if you are successful and he is lucky, he comes back to life. I can sing now with new meaning the old hymn:

> Breathe on me, breath of God
> Fill me with life anew,
> That I may love what Thou dost love,
> And do what Thou wouldst do.

That, in a nutshell, is how I believe in the Holy Spirit.

Finally, and however briefly, let us at least refer to the next phrase in the Creed: "I believe in the Holy Catholic Church", holding it in the context of our main thought. Take the words separately. "Holy" means "different", "separated out". "Catholic" means "throughout the whole". "Church" comes from a Greek adjective *kuriakos*, recognizable in the Scots word *kirk* or the German *Kirche*, and it means "belonging to the Lord". So when I say that I believe in the Holy Catholic Church I am referring to the whole great company, everywhere throughout the world, who stand out from the rest of humanity and are different, because they have accepted Jesus Christ as Lord. This cuts across all barriers of denominations, all closed systems of doctrine, every difference of worship or administration. The definition I find both searching and satisfying is in the words of Paul: "If a man does not possess the spirit of Christ, he is no Christian".

You will notice it says nothing about being episcopally confirmed, or baptized by total immersion as an adult, or acknowledging the authority of the Pope or denouncing him as anti-Christ, or any of the other differences that divide the organized Churches from each other. It takes its stand with Christ's own picture of the last judgment, where those who are *in* are the people who have shown in practical fashion Christ's own spirit of caring for the hurt and needy, and those who are irrevocably *out* are simply those who fail to show that spirit.

Paul seems to have had difficulty in distinguishing between the spirit of Christ and the Holy Spirit, and I find the same difficulty. I only know that I develop the habit of testing whether anything that happens is the work of the Holy Spirit by this touchstone: "Does this accord with the spirit of Christ?"

If you want a list of spot-checks to apply, Paul gives it: "The harvest of the Spirit is love, joy, peace, patience, kindness, goodness, fidelity, gentleness and self-control". Any individual congregation or denomination which is producing these commodities, which have such scarcity value, belongs by this definition within the Holy Catholic Church.

The finest description I know of the function of the Church declares it to be the body of Christ. I like that, because it allows of unity with difference, wide divergence co-ordinated into harmonious obedience to the head. It also reminds me of what it means to be a member. I recently visited a man in hospital whose big toe of one foot was black with gangrene; and the next time I saw him the leg was amputated below the knee. It is as dangerous as that for me to be less than a live member of the Church. The Church is in the world with a tremendous task, to get done what Christ wants done. It cannot begin to face the task unless the body is filled in every part with the life and power that can come only from the Holy Spirit.

5

ABOUT THE FORGIVENESS OF SINS

Which article in the Creed, would you think, is most difficult
for modern man to accept, goes most against the grain of his
thinking, carries the greatest element of what the New Testa
ment calls a stumbling-block?   The Virgin Birth, perhaps,
which goes dead against our current mood of dismissing any
element in life that smacks of the supernatural, and will not
fit, neatly and tidily into our biological pigeonholes?   The
descent into hell, maybe, even when we have fallen over
backwards to explain that it does not mean what it seems on
the surface to imply?   The Resurrection, quite likely, a real
stumbling-block idea in a generation which is reputed to
believe less and less in a life after death, of any sort, for
anyone, under any condition at all?   Or would the whole
concept of the Ascension be your choice for a real non-starter
in this space age when any child old enough to read the
simplest of space comics knows that heaven and God just
aren't "up there"?   I personally feel that a very strong
case could be made out for this particular article to which
we now come: "I believe in the forgiveness of sins."

Now, why should anyone say that?   For the simple and
sufficient reason that of all the sweeping generalizations made
about modern man, one of the commonest and most widely
made is that he is no longer troubled at all by a sense of sin.
This is not at all surprising when one tries to analyse the
climate of thinking in our time.   Probably the biggest single
influence has been the findings of modern psychology, progressively infiltrating the thinking of the ordinary man
throughout most of this country.

Now, it would be both ungracious and plain dishonest to
minimize in any way the manifold benefits that have accrued
to mankind from the theories propounded as to the roots of
and reasons for human behaviour, and the care with which

such theories have been tested both in depth and width. To know how the human mind works, why we do what we do, and how we become what we are, to probe the secrets of personality and all that makes for individuality can bring a man nothing but benefit and untold blessing in the form of a deeper understanding of his own nature and ability to handle it wisely, alike in its weakness and its strength. This has also quite splendidly opened up wonderful new areas of skilled, positive remedial treatment for a wide variety of people who suffer from personality defects of one sort or another, or are still more deeply handicapped. All of this is sheer gain, and we can only ask for more and better psychological research and still wider application of psychiatric remedial or even preventive treatment at all levels.

Having said this I hope it is not unfair to suggest that sometimes such research has been too exclusively analytical, like the motor mechanic who takes the engine completely to pieces till he finds the broken part, but does not put it together again. To demonstrate what is wrong does not always convey the power to put it right. Is it too utterly " square " to quote even today Studdert-Kennedy's reservations on this whole subject set down, though they were, some fifty years ago?

" The Psychologist "

He takes the saints to pieces,
And labels all the parts,
He tabulates the secrets
Of loyal, loving hearts.
He probes their selfless passion,
And shows exactly why
The martyr goes out singing,
To suffer and to die. . . .
The subtle sex perversion,
His eagle glance can tell,
That makes their joyous heaven
The horror of their hell.

His reasoning is perfect,
His proofs as plain as paint,
He has but one small weakness,
He cannot make a saint.

One feels it necessary to enter this tiny caveat to the common assumption that in this area of human knowledge are to be found "all the answers". But one must hasten to add, in all fairness, that what has developed out of all this to militate against the Christian faith and its doctrine of man and his nature, is not the fault of the psychologists and psychiatrists—blessings be upon all their works—but rather of the so-called man-in-the-street, or even the man-in-the-pew (at least occasionally), who has absorbed or gleefully seized upon some half-baked ideas of what the experts are really saying.

For example, most of us could quote at least one "mixed-up kid" in danger of growing up to be a menace to himself and to society who had a bad start with parents who refused to discipline or direct him in any way because they were so scared of repressing him and inflicting some deep traumatic experience on his delicate psyche! I am Philistine enough to be tempted to add: "For 'traumatic experience' read 'timely, richly merited and wholly beneficial smack on the behind'!"

At a much more serious level lies the widely accepted and eagerly welcomed idea that here is the scapegoat to end all scapegoats. You remember the basic idea. In biblical times the people, burdened with a sense of sin, would gather with the priest around a chosen goat. They would confess the sins of which they wished to be rid, the priest laid his hands on the back of the goat, thus symbolically transferring to the scapegoat the burden of the people's sins, and then the goat was driven out into the wilderness carrying away their sins with it. Now what could be better? My scapegoat is my own nature, for which I am not responsible, and over which I have no control. I am what I am because of instincts and urges that are part of my human heritage. My aggression which makes me in some degree cruel and violent is a hang-over from a wilder era when it was essential to survival. I do what I do because of my given make-up of personality, in its strength and weakness, and I cannot be held responsible for the results. I am sure any reputable psychologist would reject out of hand such over-simplification, but it is the way lots of people, even subconsciously, think. It is wishful thinking. If you want to get rid of any awkward sense of sin, you have made it totally irrelevant in such a climate.

Not altogether dissociated from this attitude is our right and proper emphasis on the effect of environment on personality and behaviour. We are growing rightly more and more concerned about the social conditions in which the formative years of life are spent: the kind of home, the wider community, the quality of educational opportunity. How often one reads a press report of some quite ugly case of crime where the case was continued for a week to get " a background report ".

Of course, this is essential to an understanding of what kind of person this is, what made him do what he did, and how best his case can be dealt with. What is dangerous is the assumption that you can totally explain him in terms of his background so as to diminish his responsibility for doing what he did. Here is another phoney scapegoat. I like C. A. Joyce's pithy comment: " We have got to realize that a boy will steal cigarettes because he wants to smoke, and not because someone hit his mother over the head with a cigar-box three months before he was born ! "

A third factor reducing any sense of sin in modern man is the general erosion of long-accepted standards of right and wrong. It is not only East of Suez (with apologies to all my Australian friends !) that " there ain't no Ten Command-ments ". There is only one left on the statute book: " Thou shalt not get found out ". To refer to only one most obvious area of conduct, if modern methods of contraception had been as widely available in Burns' day, the stool of repent-ance would have been empty much more often than it was, although it is a curious fact that our illegitimacy rate continues to rise. If the only governing consideration is what I can get away with, all the old-fashioned talk about sin and sinners is completely out of date. Yet, with it all, one cannot help wondering.

The whole biblical view about man and his nature and his condition is that he is a sinner needing to be saved, not from personality defects, nor from environmental handicaps, though both are real enough, but from his sins. After all, Jesus was given the name " Jesus," which as we saw earlier means Deliverer, and the object of the exercise was made quite specifically clear: " He shall save his people from their sins ". Is this really as irrelevant to the condition of modern man as we are led to believe? Does it not seem significant that in the most affluent societies, such as, say, Britain or America, where man is most able to take care of himself and with all his wealth of resources and technical know-how, is saying to God, in effect: " Anything you can do, I can do better ; I can do *anything* better than you "— it is precisely in these countries that we have a very high rate of mental and nervous illness, so many people who in various ways and in varying degrees are not able to cope. It is also in that same setting that you find the substitute religions like the gambling craze, the worship of Lady Luck, and the proliferations of the various " escape routes " like drugs, or drink leading on to the swiftly escalating disease of alcoholism, or even, in the last resort suicide.

These facts of life for modern man—for they are facts, and undeniable, whatever their explanation—are usually written down as the price we have to pay for all the tensions and pressures of modern living. Could it be that the biblical view of man is nearer the reality than we think, that Augustine is still on the mark when he bids us say to God: " Thou hast made us for Thyself, and our hearts are restless until they find their rest in Thee " ? Could it be that if we deny some basic fact of our human situation, brush aside some deep-down need of our nature, our nature itself takes revenge on us, and we end up by paying too high a price?

I am going to stick out my neck and say that I believe that if we are not right with God at the centre of life we will never be right anywhere. Having said that, let's make a fresh approach to this article in the Creed, coming at it now with a reasonably open mind: "I believe in the forgiveness of sins".

Notice, it does not say "I believe in the forgiveness of *sin*". I do not know if there was any special significance in the plural as the Creed came to take shape, but it seems to me important that we are not talking about sin in general, sin as an abstract idea, some theological theory cooked up by the pundits and used by the parsons, like Burns' "the fear o' hell's a hangman's whip to keep the wretch in order". We are not discussing something that exists only as part of the stock-in-trade of the Church to keep itself in business. We are talking about sins, real sins that actual people commit, that are part of life as we experience it, sins that spoil human relationships, that leave the person concerned with a sense of guilt and a desire to seek forgiveness, if and where it can be found. A great deal depends on how we understand the nature of sin, and of our own particular sins, whether we take all this seriously or not. Let's try to come at it gradually, by stages, in terms of words used in the Bible for "sin" or "sins".

One of the most common words, used both in the Old Testament and the New, means to miss the mark, to fall short. If you were thinking in terms of archery, and this is one of the applications of the general idea, it would mean to miss the target altogether. Now, at first sight, this might seem just another convenient scapegoat, this lets me out. Just as I might gleefully confess to being an utter rabbit at golf and still insist that I enjoy the game, so I am just a poor performer at this business of living, and it's no use you blaming me, or me blaming myself for making bad shots, for that's the way I am. But the picture here is not just so simple and easy-going as that.

The word carries the clear suggestion of making a bad shot when I had it in me to make a better one, being off the target altogether when I could easily have hit it, or being content with an " outer " when, if I had really concentrated, I could have registered at least an " inner " or maybe even a " bull ". This seems to me to provide common ground on which we can all meet together and from which we can start. You may gabble through the prayer of General Confession, and in describing yourself as one of the " miserable offenders " feel that you have nothing to be miserable about, and that by comparison with the general standard, and indeed some of your not too distant neighbours, you are not much of an offender. But go back a phrase or two, and is it not true for you to say, at the very least, " We have left undone those things which we ought to have done " ? Is there any one of us who could put hand on heart and say· " I have done everything I ought to have done, and been all that I could be, as son or daughter, brother or sister, husband or wife, father or mother, employer or employee, friend or neighbour ? " Have we not all without exception fallen short of what we might have been, what deep down we feel we ought to have been because this is what God meant us to be, even what, in our better moments we wanted to be ? We have fallen below the best we set ourselves as target, sometimes descending to our lowest, most often just being content with second best. Yes, in this real and searching sense we have all sinned and fallen short. I do not know about you, but I am perpetually haunted by the memory of the things I have not done and I will never do them now ; the people I might have helped, and they are now forever beyond my reach. I keep hoping they will forgive me but I have not got any right to expect it, and it is difficult to be sure.

The next word is more positive, for it means to cross a line, literally to " transgress " to go beyond the division between right and wrong. It carries the suggestion that I saw the line quite clearly and yet deliberately crossed. Here it is obviously relevant to remark how much the situation is complicated by the blurring of the distinction between right and wrong. When there are no clear dividing lines any more how can I know if I am transgressing, and how can I distinguish the divisions that really matter, how separate in my thinking and my decisions mere chalklines drawn on the surface by Victorian prudery or narrow, negative Puritanism, from distinctions built in to life itself?

Yet in spite of all this blurring I still reach the point where, deep down I feel: " I ought not ". So another phrase of the General Confession comes back into its own: " We have done those things which we ought not to have done ". We have, haven't we? Take this week for example. Have you any difficulty at all in remembering something you have done and wish you had not done? You wish you had not done it for you know it was wrong. If you could go back and undo it you would, but you cannot. It is woven into the web of life and you cannot run the machinery backwards and unpick it. Would you have to search very hard to find some deed done, further back, or some word spoken that must be desperately hard for the person concerned to forgive, and you have no sort of right to expect it?

If we are agreed thus far we can go on a stage further that carries us much deeper down. Surely the greatest story ever written about sin and forgiveness is the one familiar to us all as that of the Prodigal Son. It would be much more truly named the Forgiving Father. Look how badly the younger son behaved, from first to last. With what gross selfishness he claims the share of the inheritance which will be his due when his father dies, as if he could not even wait till then. How truculently he turns it all into cash and marches off, asserting his independence, claiming so rudely the right to live his own life, without the slightest thought for his father's feelings. How blatantly he lives it up in the far country, indulging in all the sins of the flesh slumped under the title of riotous living. How unworthy, really, his motives for turning homewards. Look under the surface of things, and in spite of all his pretty rehearsed speech of contrition, note that the real reason for going home was not that he was deeply repentant, but just because he was starving!

Notice what the story reveals as to what sin really does. It ruins a relationship. Even the prodigal realized that he had no right any more to be called a son or treated like one. The very best he could hope for was to be taken back as one of the hired servants, not even of the family. This is what sin does, precisely, it destroys a relationship, and nothing the sinner can possibly do can restore that relationship to what it was before. So the boy comes home, and when he is yet a long way off the father sees him, because he has been looking out for him, yearning after him ever since he left. The New English Bible says splendidly " his heart went out to him " and where his heart went his feet ran to follow.

What a changed son he saw, gone away so high and mighty, now disgraced, penniless, filthy, stinking of the pig trough, barefoot and in rags. His youth and health are gone and gone for ever. He will bear the marks of his debauchery to his dying day. No power on earth, not even God himself can cancel out what he has done as if he had not done it.

That is not what forgiveness means. But watch the father, and you will see what it *does* mean. He cuts short the speech of apology, he rolls out the red carpet for this ragged rascal, and gives him what we would describe as the V.I.P. treatment ; all to say to him that in spite of all that has happened he still treats the prodigal as his son. He restores the relationship as if it had never been broken. This is what forgiveness means. This is how God treats us. But look again, and you will realize how much forgiveness is needed, and why nothing less than this will meet the situation. Do you know when that younger son realized for the first time the full meaning of what he had done ? I believe it was when he saw his father, when he saw the marks of suffering on his father's face etched deeper every day he had been away, and the father's sense of shock, instinctively registering because of his love for his son when he saw how he came

(handwritten margin note at top: "give th boys money we give. He had nothing left to pay... Licence. So give.")

back. It was only then he got to the heart of what he had done, what his sins really meant, how he had hurt his father.

This is fundamental to any understanding of the real nature of what sin does ; no, what your sins and mine do. Someone always gets hurt ; the person against whom I sin and myself, and God ; others, too, very often in ever widening circles of chain reaction effect.

In Dorothy Sayers' famous play sequence for radio *The Man Born to be King* there is a scene where the risen Christ meets with his disciples after his Resurrection. After the first joy and wonder are over, some appalling implications dawn on these men. Peter asks, " Master when I disowned you . . . when we disbelieved and doubted you . . . when we failed and deserted and betrayed you . . . is that what we do to God ? " Jesus answers, " Yes, Peter ". James goes on, " Lord, when they mocked and insulted and spat at you . . . when they flogged you . . . when they howled for your blood . . . when they nailed you to the Cross and killed you . . . is that what we do to God ? " " Yes, James ", replies Jesus. Then John, who always saw deeper than the others, asks the glorious final question. Drawing the unbelievable but only possible conclusion, he goes on as if he did not need to be answered: " Beloved, when you patiently suffered all things, and went down to death with all our sins heaped upon you . . . is that what God does for us ? "

We are at the very heart of the matter now. We never understand what our falling short means, why our transgressions matter, until we see what they do to God. We never begin to realize how wonderful is the forgiveness of sins until we see what God does for us, and at what cost. To take forgiveness for granted, to accept it casually, for anyone who has ever come anywhere near the Cross is quite unthinkable. One question remains. Are we forgiven unconditionally ? The honest answer is both Yes and No. God sets no conditions to forgiving us, but even he cannot forgive us unless we recognize our need for forgiveness and really want to be forgiven. The one condition of forgiveness, God being

what he has shown himself to be in Jesus Christ, and we
being what we show ourselves to be when we sin, is repent-
ance. To repent means literally " to think again, to change
our minds, and so to want to be different ". Real repentance
is costly.

As Chairman of the Parole Board for Scotland I have to
read a lot of case histories of people who have clearly sinned,
against society, often grievously against others, always also
against themselves. They have committed crimes like
violent assault, rape, theft, or embezzlement on a large scale,
culpable homicide, murder even. One category in the case
sheet is headed " Attitude to the Offence " and the reactions
vary widely. Some persistently and in face of all the evidence go on protesting their innocence. Some just couldn't
care less. Some are sorry they got caught and are having to
pay for what they did. Some are filled with remorse, shocked
by the picture, printed for ever on their memory, of the
dreadful injuries they inflicted in their insensate violence,
sometimes on a complete stranger. Many a one is deeply
repentant of the wrong he has done, both to the victim and
his family and to his own wife and family who are very dear
to him. When a man is repentant to that degree he is a good
risk. He is not likely to offend again. He wants too badly
to be different. That is the degree of repentance the Cross
as nothing else produces in me, it makes me want to be
different.

When any thinking man gets near enough to the Cross he
knows himself to be judged. We have said nothing about
the question of judgment. We had not time to go into all the
problems raised by the idea of the Second Coming or to ask
what we mean when we say " From thence he shall come to
judge the quick and the dead ". The idea of the Second
Coming is central, crucial and urgent for some Christians ;
for others it may seem to stand on the circumference of faith.
At the very least it stands for this : that history is not just
going round in a vicious spiral, it is making for a climax
and that is the ultimate triumph of Christ and all he stands

E

for.   On the element of judgment one can at least say that
this Jesus keeps on coming to us, here and now, and just by
his being there we are judged.

   Studdert-Kennedy has a poem in which an old soldier
dismisses the idea of a judgment throne, and books which
contain a man's record, and ends up:

> It's 'Im, just 'Im, that is the Judge
> Of blokes like you and me.
> And, boys, I'd sooner frizzle up,
> I' the flames of a burnin' 'Ell,
> Than stand and look into 'Is face,
> And 'ear 'Is voice say—" Well ? "

That old soldier was right, and that's why I am so profoundly
glad I can say: " I believe in the forgiveness of sins ".

6

ABOUT THE LIFE EVERLASTING

It is time to step back and take a look at what we have been thinking. I hope some of us at least will come to believe together.

I recently had the interesting experience of having my portrait painted and found it quite fascinating at every stage to watch how the artist went about his job. He spent the whole of the first morning simply working out the position in which he wanted me to sit, moving me about on his raised platform, altering the angle of the chair in relation to the light from the big skylight window overhead, fiddling about with curtains flung over a draughtscreen, to alter the reflection of light. When he was finally satisfied he made chalk-marks on the floor for the position of the dais, and round the legs of the chair, so that the setting would always be the same, the relationship to the light would not alter. As he worked, every now and then he would step back from the painting on the easel, take a good, searching look at his victim, then add a touch of this, a brush stroke of that. Sometimes he would rub off what did not satisfy him and start again. From no more than a rough outline the portrait took shape and came alive in a quite fascinating way, and when he had finished, lo and behold, he had answered, for me at least, Burns' famous prayer: " O wad some po'er the giftie gie us, to see oorsels as ithers see us ! "

All this is not just a bit of personal chit-chat but relevant and important before we move on to the final stage. What we have been doing is carrying out very much this same process. Out of all our thinking has been emerging for each of us a portrait of myself, my own life, my place in the world, my nature, my worth, what I am here to be and to do. We have set that picture all along in the light of our knowledge of the glory of God as revealed in Jesus Christ, we have kept looking from different angles at what God has done for us in

Jesus Christ, and what he keeps on doing. We have come with an inevitable feeling of growing humility and an ever-increasing sense of wonder to see ourselves, our little, blundering unimportant lives as God sees us. Now we are at the stage of stepping back and looking at the total effect.

Just to keep us right let's sprinkle a few stars in the background of the picture to remind us where we started, how great is the God who takes so much trouble over us. Then let's take a long, hard look at the total effect. If God has gone to such lengths to save us, to set us free, to give to us, in Christ, life to the full ; if Christ is still at work in our world ; if the Holy Spirit is constantly breathing into us new life to equip us to serve God's purpose, then don't we need somehow to put the whole picture in the setting of an eternal hope ? How are we to relate all this to the one universal, inescapable fact of death ?

We are really bracketing together three of the final phrases of the Creed: " I believe in the Communion of Saints ... the Resurrection of the body and the Life Everlasting ". We are clearly entering here into a particularly difficult area of thought and belief, trying to picture that of which we can have no knowledge, to describe the indescribable.

Let me tell you, quite simply, how I approach the problem. Remember that all I am trying to say comes not out of any theoretical or abstract approach, but out of the practical experience of facing the reality of death, which comes to anyone who in forty years has seen some of his own nearest and dearest die, and has shared with hundreds of people of all sorts, as their minister, in facing death when it came to them, or, more trying still, has tried to help their loved ones who are left, shattered as they must be by the grim finality of death and parting.

Over the years I have come to find myself more and more centring my thoughts and building my faith in relation to the fact of death, less and less on the Resurrection of Jesus himself, as the supreme test case, the key event, and more and more on two great realities which have continually emerged during the whole of our study, and which are indeed seen, raised to the nth power, as it were, in the Cross and Easter Day. I picture these two realities, the wisdom and the love of God, as the twin towers of a bridge that supports and sustains my faith and makes possible my belief in the life everlasting.

There are two famous bridges, familiar to us all in reality or in countless photographs. One is the Forth Road Bridge. It is made possible by its tall twin towers. The foundations of the one on the south side go right down 100 feet below the bed of the river. Those for its twin needed to go down only 30 feet to the levelled-out solidity of the Mackintosh Rock. On these firm foundations rise the towers fully 500 feet high. Over the top are slung the great cables, spun out of fine steel wire, that carry the bridge, holding it up, anchored firmly at either end.

The other bridge is the world-famous Sydney Harbour Bridge. It works on almost exactly the opposite principle with its great single arch buttressed at either end by the two great towers, each of which looks like two because of the smaller towers that rise on either side of the roadway; but below roadlevel each is a great solid block to contain the downward thrust of the arch.

Anyway, here is the principle from which I start my thinking, a bridge strong enough to carry my faith, my hopes, all that my mind and heart demand about another life to which we may look forward beyond this one, and it all rests on the two great realities of the wisdom and the love of God.

Suppose we start with the great final phrase of the Creed, for it involves the rest: "I believe in the Life Everlasting". The world translated "everlasting" is a very important one for all our thinking; it describes not extent in time—"lasting for ever"—but rather life of a special quality. The two are not of course inseparable, but it is the emphasis that is important. If you buy a dining-room table made of solid mahogany by a real craftsman it will last you a lifetime; if you settle for a mass-produced affair made of plywood and

veneer it won't last ; but it is the quality that is decisive.
Notice further, that we speak about the Life Everlasting, not
just Life Everlasting. One doesn't want to make too much
of this but it is suggestive. We are talking about a particular
kind of life that has a special quality. Now turn to the New
Testament and you will find that " life everlasting " is almost
invariably referred to, not as something that may be con-
ferred upon us, as gift or reward, after we are dead—" Pie in
the sky when you die " to use the ugly, familiar caricature—
but as a present possession, something we can have and enjoy
here and now. " He that believeth on me *hath* everlasting
life," says Jesus ; and John writes, " We know that we have
passed from death unto life "—already, here and now, in this
life—" because we love the brethren."

I believe, on the basis of the New Testament, that when
this Jesus Christ becomes a reality in my life, the central
reality, when I accept him as Saviour and seek to obey and
serve him as Lord, I have entered into a new relationship
with God through him, I am living a life of a different nature
and a particular quality which can be described at this
moment as " everlasting ". I can only go on to insist that
the mere fact of my physical death will not break that
relationship, nor make any difference at all to that onward-
going life.

This, to me, makes sense, as I rest my faith and hope on
my twin towers of reality. I hold with Paul that " neither
death nor life, nor things present, nor things to come shall
be able to separate us from the love of God which is in
Christ Jesus our Lord ". The Cross was the test for this,
for it proved that not even death can defeat the love of God.
Often, in the face of stark, unrelieved tragedy this is the only
reality that stands firm. One of the hardest parts of seeing
a loved one die is the ruthless inevitability of it. All human
skill is not enough to prevent that life slipping through the
fingers of your love ; death is inexorably prizing them open
and you must let go. But it is precisely at that point that
most surely and firmly the love of God holds fast. I believe

in the life everlasting because I believe to this extent in the love of God.

But equally I rest on my other tower, the wisdom of God. The whole story of our faith which we have been thinking about has revealed increasingly the unsearchable wisdom of this God in whom we believe. Start with the mystery of the universe, from the beginning of all things when, in the great, glowing phrase, " the morning stars sang together and all the sons of God shouted for joy ". Think of the long slow aeons in which the world as we see it and life as we know and live it came to be. Look at the skill both in grand strategy and attention to detail with which God's great plan of salvation was conceived and carried out. Marvel at the resource of God, revealed in the Cross and the Resurrection, whereby the wrath of man was made to praise him. Follow down the ages the growth of the Church. Look at the skill with which God's power has worked in your own life, and maybe already you can bless the hand that guided so wisely and the heart that planned with such skill.

I believe that God is wise beyond our understanding. I cannot see such a God planning our whole lives and then being caught unawares by the fact of our death ; saying in effect, " I never thought of that ". I cannot accept that, any more than I could accept that any competent civil engineer would build a huge steel bridge and not allow for expansion and contraction in hot sunshine or sub-zero temperatures ; watch his brain-child twist and warp, or even crash with a load of lives, and blandly write it off with a mystified: " I'm sorry. I never thought of that ".

I believe in a God who is at least as clever and knowledgeable as the men who planned and built Sydney Bridge and the Forth Road Bridge, or the engineers who tunnelled so exactly through the Snowy Mountains, or the great team of experts who have put men on the moon. I believe that, just as they do, he has calculated all the strains and stresses, and looked at and provided for every situation that will have to be met. I believe that God has planned for death, and made his careful preparations for something more beyond.

It is part of wisdom not to be wasteful and I believe that God is wise enough not to waste precious material. This is to me a most cogent argument in many cases. Some time ago a young neuro-surgeon had been on duty for several nights in succession. He was called out to a hospital to operate on an accident victim brought in from the dangerous three-lane highway between Edinburgh and Glasgow. He went, concentrated keenly as he had to on the delicate operation that had to be performed, and set out in what we call " the wee, sma' 'oors " of the night to drive home. Not surprisingly he fell asleep at the wheel, crashed and was killed. What a waste of potential, of skill just coming to its finest, of all that he might have gone on to do for suffering mankind. How often we come across cases like this, of some life full of promise or rich in experience, highly valuable, needed, useful, being suddenly cut off. It seems appallingly, gratuitously wasteful. And what of the much wider field, of the many people who, not so much perhaps by some special skill, but by the sheer radiant quality of their lives, make it impossible to accept that they should be wiped out as if they had never been ? I am not suggesting that there is going to be a need for neuro-surgeons in heaven. I am only insisting that God is wise enough not to be wasteful of so much that is of lasting worth even in this life.

If then, we agree thus far, that there is good ground for believing that the life everlasting can be a glorious reality, what can we say about its nature ? Where, for example, is heaven ? Let's recognize quite honestly that we are talking about something we cannot even begin to describe. All the pictures in the familiar hymns are only pictures doing their best to express what breaks through language and thought and eludes our grasp. I think of heaven not as a place, but rather a condition, the condition of being in a new nearness to God, in a life of new freedom, where all that has been best here in this life will be better still. I will try to define more closely what I mean by that in a moment. At present, let me enter a protest against the " image " contained in one familiar hymn.

Those of us who are older sang blithely when we were children: " There is a happy land, far, far away ". This seems to me to be dangerous nonsense. Wherever and whatever heaven is, it is not far away. If being in heaven means being near to God, then it surely stands to reason that we who are left on earth, whenever we are near to God are wonderfully near also to those whom we have loved and lost awhile and who are nearer to God than we are.

We have now reached the stage when we can, and indeed must, begin to ask what we can believe about the nature of life, life of this special quality, unbroken by the act of physical death, and continuing under new conditions of freedom. The reference we have just made to physical death brings us right up against that most awkward clause in the Creed, the clause so many people find offensive both to intelligence and feeling: " I believe in the Resurrection of the body ".

The scholars tell us that this idea was put into the Creed to contradict some dangerous opposite opinions that were held in the formative centuries of Christian belief, such as the Greek idea of the immortality of the soul, or the proposition that the body was essentially evil and beyond redemption, that " this muddy vesture of decay " was a prison from which the spirit needed to be set free. It was also inserted for positive reasons, like the insistence that God's saving power extends to the whole man, body, mind and spirit, or the underlining of the implications of the Incarnation, that God uniquely revealed himself by becoming bone of our bone and flesh of our flesh, and that the physical part of our nature is thereby touched and for ever dignified. Whatever the reasons for it, there can be no doubt that it raises great difficulties especially for the modern mind. One of the troubles is that it can be stated with a crude kind of literalism that can totally obscure the real meaning of the doctrine.

Let me employ the method of indirect proof we used to

use in the geometry class and called *reductio ad absurdum.*
Let's suppose that several years ago a miner was trapped by
a fall of rock in the narrow gallery of a coal mine. The
rescuers fought their way through and found him firmly
gripped by the leg among piles of rock which could not be
moved at all without the entire roof crashing down, as it was
likely to do any moment in any case. The only way to save
the man's life was for the doctor to operate on the spot, even
in these very difficult conditions and amputate his leg, and
this was successfully achieved. No sooner were the man and
his rescuers safely clear than the whole gallery collapsed and
the mine was thereafter closed, as being too dangerous for
further working. Meantime the miner recovered from this
shocking ordeal, grew accustomed to managing with an
artificial leg, abidingly grateful to be alive at all, lived to a
ripe old age, and was buried in a country kirkyard, or more
likely cremated. At some far-off resurrection day the physical atoms of the severed leg, long since mouldered away
deep down in the bowels of the earth, and of the rest of the
tired old body are re-assembled, and the whole man appears
before God.

This is the kind of thing that makes arrant nonsense and
flies in the face of all our bitter experience of the grim
finality of death. I can only bear witness to the fact that I
have never looked on the dead body of someone I have
really known without feeling that the real person is no longer
there ; this is only the empty house from which the tenant is
departed ; there is nothing so completely dead as a dead
human body. Time after time I am thankful for that feeling ;
when I think of how I have seen so many die of cancer, the
body breaking down completely, I can only thank God he
has not chosen to tie our souls to an immortal body. In very
few cases that I can remember, would one want the body to
come back as it was.

Does that mean we are driven back as the only alternative
on something so shadowy and insubstantial as the immortality of the soul, whatever we may take that to mean ? Not

if we can rediscover the great positive idea so often covered up by the misrepresentation of this doctrine. How I wish that everyone would read carefully what Paul says on this topic in 1 Corinthians, 15, where he develops his idea of another body. I find it most helpful, and it brings me back again to my tower-like reality, the wisdom of God. When I look at the sheer walking miracle of this body God has given us in this life, it is no great leap of faith to believe He might be capable of devising another body adapted to totally different conditions of life, yet still performing certain essential functions.

Let me suggest some of these. I believe in the continuance of individuality. It is my faith that in that other life I will remain me, you will remain you; that just as in this life we recognize our own by outward physical characteristics, height, build, certain facial features, the tones of a voice, some distinctive trick or gesture, so we shall be provided with the means of establishing our identity, continuing our recognizable, personal, individual existence. I say that for two reasons. First because one of the greatest marvels in this life is our individuality, with all we can contribute to the life of others because we are so different from each other, and I do not think a wise God will waste that. Still more important, I believe that the richest gift God has given us in this life is love, his love for us and our human love for each other, and I do not believe that a God of love will allow that gift to be blotted out or deny it the opportunity of expression. I cling to the hope that those who have known and loved each other best will be together again, able to recognize and greet each other, to share in love that fuller life as they shared this one in love.

I believe in the continuance of service and activity. I do not believe in the description of the afterlife given in the old hymn " And then to rest for ever." If you are alive at all— I trust we shall be more alive than ever—to rest for ever, to do nothing at all for ever and ever, would not be heaven ; it would be hell! The greatest joy in this life is to be found in using our strength and skill in service to our fellows and to God. I like far better the picture of being called to a higher service and provided with the means of rendering such service, as in this life we do with hands and hearts and minds and voices.

I also believe in the continuance of growth and development. Another of the many marvels of this present life is the way we grow, all the way from the original wonder of conception, through birth and the dawn of self-conscious personality to maturity, and keep on growing in experience even when the body is only growing old. This I would stress for three reasons. Think of the practical implications of what we have just said about being together again with those we love. What of the mother who loses a six-year-old child in a road accident. Slowly, painfully she adjusts herself, for life must go on, but she never forgets. She finally dies, an old woman. Does she meet a child of six? Or, from another point of view, in that same situation, would it be either wise or loving of God to leave a child at that stage, denied the opportunity of development, of enjoying the splendour of growing up into fulness of life? And what about the very many people who never had a chance in this life, who for one reason or another never heard the message of God's love, never had the choice presented to them? Does our sense of bare justice not demand an opportunity to go on growing and developing?

It is an interesting fact that the word in John 14 translated "mansions" in the famous verse "In my Father's house are many mansions" can mean, quite literally, "resting places for the night", such as a youth hostel, where you come in the evening and spend the night sleeping in its shelter and security, but you get up in the morning and go on your journey. I like to think there will be many new mornings, many challenging new starts on fresh stages of the journey.

I think of all that when we state: "I believe in the Resurrection of the body". So, working back the way, we come to the Communion of Saints. Notice that for this purpose we have moved this phrase one place out of context, for it comes immediately after the belief in the Holy Catholic Church. It was placed there in the Creed because when we speak of the Communion of Saints we are just looking to the Church in heaven. It is one Church, triumphant in heaven, striving, struggling here on earth. At a personal level the Church is one family circle, still unbroken, in heaven and on earth. This is a wonderful thought. One of the most tragic aspects of bereavement is the element of being cut off, out of touch ; the line has gone dead and you cannot get through. People sometimes ask me if I think our dead dear ones know, from their side of things, what is happening to us who are left. I can only answer that I believe so, and that I, person- ally, find it both comforting and challenging.

Think of a young mother whose husband dies suddenly and she is left to bring up the family being both mother and father to them. She goes back to her old job, and courage- ously manages somehow. What an inspiration to think that he knows how bravely she is facing the situation, rejoicing in her fortitude and faith as she carries the double burden on his behalf, understands and shares her occasional spells of devastating loneliness, her aching for his presence.

How splendid it is that God for our comfort grants us now and then some sense of their continuing nearness, some tiny reassurance that they are never far off. Things happen which feel like the touch of familiar hands. The Communion of Saints is a glorious idea, but it is not always a comfortable one. What a stark challenge it can be sometimes, and how badly needed, especially if we have allowed ourselves to sink into an abyss of self-pity, just letting life tumble in about us, daring to " grudge our loved one sair tae the land o' the leal " as the old Scots song puts it. There is a kind of total, collapsed grieving that can be the worst kind of disloyalty to the one who is gone.

There is one last question which someone may well be asking, out of the background of our current bewilderment with new ideas and the wide uncertainty of belief, not least in this particular area. All this that we have been saying seems to arise out of the idea of a special relationship to God in Jesus Christ and would appear to be confined to those who have accepted him as Saviour and are following him as Lord. Does that mean that there is an after life only for those and such as those? What about those who have never thought about things, or the honest doubters, or the seekers who admire Jesus as a great and good man but cannot go the whole way?

It is quite clear that no one has the right to play about with the chance he has been given, and then almost casually ask for another. More important, remember we have been talking all along in the setting of the wisdom and the love of God, and I would never dare to set limits to either, or to say that anyone is beyond the saving reach of that love which has been rightly described as the greatest thing in the world.